FOSSIL FUELS

EARLY BIRD EARTH SCIENCE

BY CONRAD J. STORAD

LERNER PUBLICATIONS COMPANY • MINNEAPOLIS

To Rohn and Michael.
Teach my grandchildren to respect the beauty of the environment and to practice conservation.

The photographs in this book are used with the permission of: PhotoDisc Royalty Free by Getty Images, pp. 1 (title type), 34, backgrounds on pp. 1, 6, 12, 21, 34, 44, 45, 46, 47; © Jose Luis Roca/AFP/Getty Images, pp. 4, 40; © Tim Graham/Getty Images, p. 5; © Karlene Schwartz, pp. 6, 10, 14, 24, 32, 39; © John Sohlden/Visuals Unlimited, p. 7; © Veer George Diebold/Photonica/Getty Images, p. 8; © Emmanuel Faure/SuperStock, p. 9; © age fotostock/SuperStock, pp. 11, 30, 31, 37, 38, 41, 46, 47, 48 (bottom); © Arthur R. Hill/Visuals Unlimited, p. 12; © Ken Lucas/Visuals Unlimited, pp. 13, 15; © Lowell Georgia/Corbis, p. 16; © Larry Lee Photography/CORBIS, p. 17; © Inga Spence/Visuals Unlimited, pp. 19, 43, 48 (top); © Bill Barley/SuperStock, p. 20; © Floyd Dean/Taxi/Getty Images, p. 21; © Tom Adams/Visuals Unlimited, p. 22; © Wim van Egmond/Visuals Unlimited, p. 23; © Jonathan S. Blair/National Geographic/Getty Images, p. 25; © Dr. Dennis Kunkel/Visuals Unlimited, p. 26; © Scott Nelson/Reportage/Getty Images, p. 27; © Scott Nelson/Stringer/Getty Images, p. 28; © Prisma/SuperStock, p. 29; © Krystyna Borgen/Independent Picture Service, p. 33; © Robert Nickelsberg/Time & Life Pictures/Getty Images, p. 35; © SuperStock, Inc./SuperStock, p. 36; © Dwight Ellefsen/SuperStock, p. 42.

Front cover: © Bob Sacha/Corbis
Front cover title type: PhotoDisc Royalty Free by Getty Images
Back cover: © Reuters/CORBIS
Illustration on p. 18 by © Laura Westlund/Lerner Publishing Group, Inc.

Lerner Publications Company
A division of Lerner Publishing Group, Inc.
241 First Avenue North
Minneapolis, MN 55401 U.S.A.

Website address: www.lernerbooks.com

Library of Congress Cataloging-in-Publication Data

Storad, Conrad J.
    Fossil fuels / by Conrad J. Storad.
        p.   cm. — (Early bird Earth science)
    Includes index.
    ISBN 978-0-8225-6736-3 (lib. bdg. : alk. paper)
    1. Fossil fuels—Juvenile literature. I. Title.
TP318.3.S76 2008
662'.6—dc22   2006038445

Manufactured in the United States of America
1 2 3 4 5 6 – JR – 13 12 11 10 09 08

CONTENTS

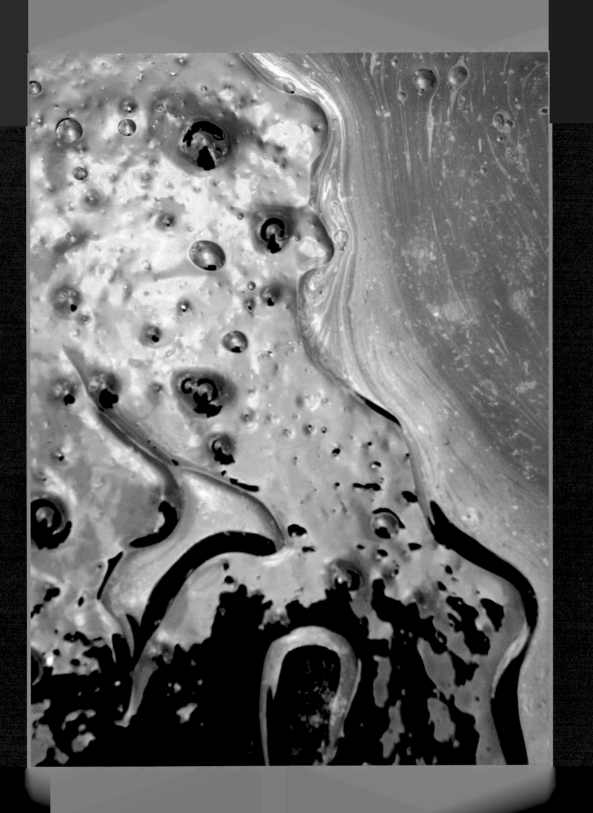

BE A WORD DETECTIVE

Can you find these words as you read about fossil fuels? Be
a detective and try to figure out what they mean. You can
turn to the glossary on page 46 for help.

bacteria	fossil	petroleum
carbon dioxide	global warming	plankton
climate	natural gas	pollution
coal	nonrenewable	remains
diatoms	nutrients	sediments

Gasoline is fuel for cars and trucks. What is fuel?

CHAPTER 1
WHAT ARE FOSSIL FUELS?

Fuel is a substance that gives things energy. It powers things. It helps them run. Fossil fuels are fuels made from fossils. Fossils are the hardened remains of ancient plants or animals.

Fossil fuels are an important source of energy. Coal is one kind of fossil fuel. Petroleum (puh-TROH-lee-uhm) is another. Petroleum is also called oil. Natural gas is a third kind of fossil fuel.

People in China used coal as fuel more than 3,000 years ago.

We get energy from fossil fuels by burning them. Burning fossil fuels gives us energy to make electricity. Electricity is the power we use to light our homes and schools. It also runs our television sets and microwave ovens.

Fossil fuels bring light to homes and other buildings.

Cars use large amounts of fossil fuels.

Burning fossil fuels helps us get from place to place. Fossil fuels make cars run. They power buses, airplanes, trains, and ships.

Some people burn fossil fuels to cook their food. Others burn them to make hot water for the shower or bath. Burning fossil fuels also helps us heat our homes.

Water heaters make cold water toasty warm. Does your home or school have a water heater?

Natural gas powers some stove tops. Other stoves use electricity.

Fossil fuels are very important. They give us energy for many things. Let's take a closer look at fossil fuels.

CHAPTER 2
COAL

Coal is a fuel most people use daily. Coal is a hard, black material. A piece of coal looks a lot like a rock.

There are three main types of coal. One type is called lignite (LIHG-nite). Lignite is the softest kind of coal. It is very crumbly.

People burn lignite to make electricity.

Bituminous (bih-TOOM-ihn-uhs) coal is the second type. Bituminous coal is harder than lignite.

The third type of coal is called anthracite (AHN-thrah-site). Anthracite is the hardest type of coal. It gives off lots of heat when it burns.

Bituminous coal is common in North America. So is another type of coal, called subbituminous (sub-bih-TOOM-ihn-uhs). Subbituminous coal is in a category between bituminous coal and lignite.

Like all coal, anthracite is made from ancient plants.

All coal is made from the remains of plants. The plants lived and died millions of years ago. How did the plants turn into coal?

Long before dinosaurs lived on Earth, murky swamps covered the land. Giant ferns, trees, and other plants covered the ground.

Over time, some of the plants died. They fell into the swamp. They sank down into the cloudy waters.

Coal formed beneath the murky waters of swamps.

It took millions of years for coal to form.

The plants fell to the bottom of the swamp. There, dirt and mud buried them. Years passed, and more plants died. These plants also fell into the swamp. Layers of dirt and mud buried them too. This went on for a very long time.

The layers of dirt and mud were squashed by the weight of all the layers above them. The weight pressed on the dead plants. At the same time, heat from inside Earth cooked the plants. The process took millions of years. The heat and pressure changed the plants into thick layers of fossils. We call these fossils coal.

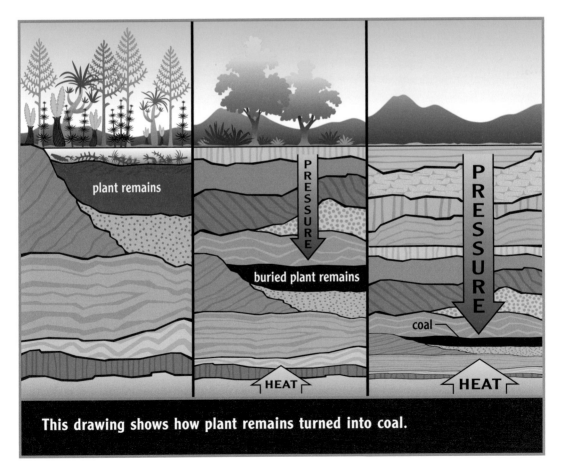

plant remains

PRESSURE

buried plant remains

HEAT

PRESSURE

coal

HEAT

This drawing shows how plant remains turned into coal.

People dig pits called mines to get to coal. This mine is in Wyoming.

Coal took a long time to form. And it took people many years to discover the fuel. But once people found coal, they quickly began putting it to use.

People once used coal to power trains. They used it to fuel ships and large machines.

Most people don't use coal for these things anymore. But we still use a lot of coal. Power plants burn coal to make electricity. People use the electricity in their homes, schools, and businesses.

Power plants, such as this one, supply buildings with electricity.

Oil is a liquid. Natural gas is a vapor. What is a vapor?

CHAPTER 3
OIL AND NATURAL GAS

Oil and natural gas are other kinds of fossil fuels. Oil is a liquid. It is black and very sticky. Natural gas is a vapor. A vapor is a thing that has no shape or texture. You cannot see or touch it.

Oil and natural gas formed in almost the same way. They formed from ocean creatures called plankton (PLANGK-tuhn) and diatoms (DIE-ah-tohms). Plankton and diatoms are very tiny. Most are no larger than the head of a pin. Some are even smaller than a period at the end of a sentence.

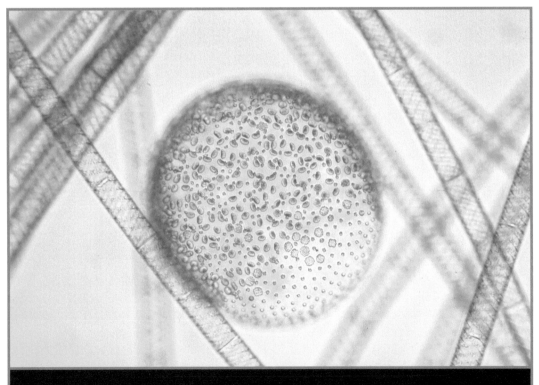

Phytoplankton (fie-toh-PLANGK-tuhn) is one type of plankton. Phytoplankton are plants.

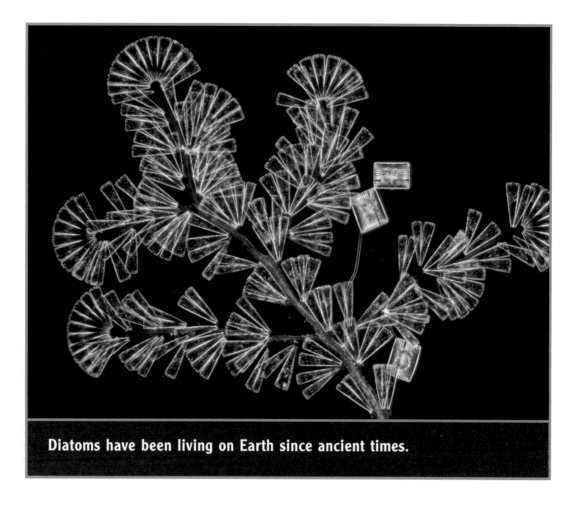

Diatoms have been living on Earth since ancient times.

Plankton and diatoms lived in ancient oceans. When ancient plankton and diatoms died, their remains drifted to the ocean floor. The remains built up over time. Soon there were billions and billions of remains. The remains formed layers on the ocean floor.

Sediments (SEH-duh-mehnts) covered the remains. Sediments are bits of sand, mud, stone, and shells. The sediments formed layers too.

Sediment layers build up over time. They can form large piles.

It takes millions of years for plant and animal remains to become fossils.

The sediment layers protected the remains. They kept the remains from rotting. This went on for millions of years. Earth's climate changed many times during all those years. Climate is a pattern of weather.

Sometimes Earth got very cold. Other times it got hot. Sometimes the oceans dried up. Then the sediments turned into stone. The stone formed a hard shell around the remains. It turned the remains into a layer of fossils.

How did the fossils turn into oil and natural gas? Scientists are not exactly sure. But most scientists think bacteria (back-TEER-ee-ah) had something to do with it.

Bacteria are tiny living creatures. They live all over Earth. They even live under sediments at the bottom of the ocean. Bacteria take nutrients (NOO-tree-uhnts) from their environments. Nutrients are chemicals that all plants and animals need to live.

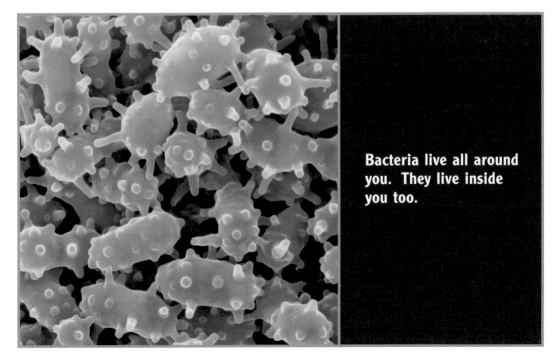

Bacteria live all around you. They live inside you too.

Bacteria turned plankton and diatoms into a thick, gooey substance.

Some bacteria took nutrients from dead plankton and diatoms. The creatures' remains turned into a layer of dark liquid.

The sediments around the liquid squeezed it very tightly. Earth's heat cooked the goo. The heat and squeezing turned the liquid into petroleum.

Pressure and high temperatures helped create huge pools of petroleum.

Pure natural gas has no color—but the fuel takes on a blue tint when it burns.

In some places, Earth was very hot. The petroleum kept on cooking. The sediment layers kept squeezing the petroleum. When this happened, some of the petroleum turned into natural gas.

People use oil and natural gas in many ways. Oil is our most important fossil fuel. People use oil to make gasoline. They use gasoline to fuel cars and trucks.

Gas stations sell gasoline to drivers. Gasoline is made from the fossil fuel oil.

Can you imagine how much gasoline these cars use?

Cars and trucks use a lot of oil. And there are millions of cars and trucks in the United States. If you lined them all up, the line would stretch from your home all the way to the moon and back!

People also use oil to make many products. They use it to make ink and plastic. They use it to make crayons and bubble gum.

Plastic jugs are made from oil. Do you use any products made from oil?

Many homes use natural gas furnaces.

Natural gas is almost as important as oil. Natural gas is a good fuel for making heat. Lots of furnaces burn natural gas. People use furnaces to heat their homes when the weather is cold.

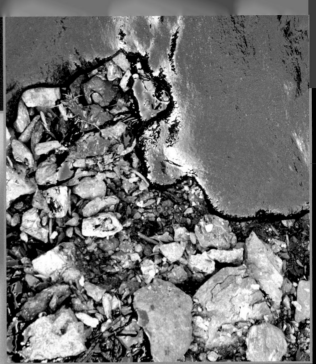

Fossil fuels are very useful, but they cause some problems. Can you name one problem with fossil fuels?

CHAPTER 4
FUEL FOR THE FUTURE

Fossil fuels are excellent sources of energy. But they will not last forever. Fossil fuels disappear when we burn them. And fossil fuels are nonrenewable (nohn ree-NEW-ah-buhl). That means that they cannot be made again. Once we use them up, they will be gone.

Pollution makes Earth's temperature rise.

If too much carbon dioxide gets into the air, heat gets trapped near Earth. The sun shines on Earth. Some of the sun's heat escapes into the atmosphere. But carbon dioxide stops the heat from escaping. It keeps the heat near Earth. This can make Earth's temperature rise. Scientists use the words *global warming* to describe Earth's rising temperature.

If Earth's temperature rises too much, cold parts of the world begin to grow warmer. Ice at the North Pole and South Pole begins to melt. Seas and oceans start to rise. These things are not good for Earth's plants and animals.

Glaciers are big, moving chunks of snow and ice. Glaciers melt when Earth's temperature warms.

Workers use pumps like this to remove oil from the ground.

Fossil fuels can be harmful in another way too. Fossil fuels lie under the ground. Some are in ground below the oceans. Workers must dig into the ground to collect coal, oil, and natural gas.

Digging into the ground disrupts the land. It can harm soil, plants, and animals. Oil spills can pollute the oceans. Workers must be very careful when digging for fossil fuels.

Ships carry oil from place to place. But sometimes, the oil spills out of the ships. It washes onto beaches.

Many scientists hope to find cleaner sources of energy.

Fossil fuels are useful. But they have some harmful effects. Scientists are working to find new and better ways to make the energy we need.

Wind can be used to make energy. So can waves or running water. The sun is another good source of energy. Lots of people are studying ways to use the power of sunlight. It is clean, and there is plenty of it.

Do you see the rectangles on this home's roof? They are called solar panels. Solar panels collect energy from the sun.

Spinning windmills use wind to make electricity.

Fossil fuels are important. But they won't last forever. We need to find new, cleaner sources of energy. By doing our part to save energy, we can help make the world a better place for everyone.

LEARN MORE ABOUT
FOSSIL FUELS

BOOKS

Petersen, Christine. *Alternative Energy.* New York: Children's Press, 2004. Learn how we can get energy from wind, sun, and water.

Stille, Darlene R. *Energy.* Chanhassen, MN: Child's World, 2005. Discover where energy comes from, how people use it, and why it is important to save energy.

Walker, Sally M. *Fossils.* Minneapolis: Lerner Publications Company, 2007. Read all about fossils—the source for fossil fuels.

Zemlicka, Shannon. *From Oil to Gas.* Minneapolis: Lerner Publications Company, 2003. Find out how oil turns into gasoline.

WEBSITES

Climate Change Kids Site
http://www.epa.gov/climatechange/kids
At this site, you can learn about climate change. You can also read about steps you can take to save energy and help the planet.

Dr. E's Energy Lab
http://www1.eere.energy.gov/kids
Dr. E leads you to links on solar energy, wind energy, alternative fuels, and more.

Energy Kid's Page
http://www.eia.doe.gov/kids
This site includes facts about energy, fun activities related to energy, and information on the history of energy.

GLOSSARY

bacteria (back-TEER-ee-ah): tiny living creatures that are made up of just one cell. They take nutrients from their environments.

carbon dioxide (CAHR-buhn dye-OK-side): a colorless, odorless gas that is released when we burn coal or oil. If too much carbon dioxide gets into the air, Earth's temperature could rise.

climate: a pattern of weather

coal: a kind of fossil fuel. The three main types of coal are lignite (LIHG-nite), bituminous (bih-TOOM-ihn-uhs), and anthracite (AHN-thrah-site) coal.

diatoms (DIE-ah-tohms): tiny ocean creatures. Remains from diatoms helped create petroleum and natural gas.

fossil: the hardened traces or remains of an ancient plant or animal

global warming: the slow rise in Earth's temperature

natural gas: a kind of fossil fuel. Natural gas is a vapor. A vapor has no shape or texture.

nonrenewable (nohn ree-NEW-ah-buhl): something that cannot be made again. Fossil fuels are nonrenewable.

nutrients (NOO-tree-uhnts): chemicals that all plants and animals need to live

petroleum (puh-TROH-lee-uhm): a kind of fossil fuel. Petroleum is a black, sticky liquid. Petroleum is also called oil.

plankton (PLANGK-tuhn): tiny ocean plants and animals. Remains from plankton helped create petroleum and natural gas.

pollution (puh-LOO-shuhn): making the air, soil, and water dirty

remains: parts left behind after plants or animals die

sediments (SEH-duh-mehnts): bits of sand, mud, stone, and shells

INDEX

Pages listed in **bold** type refer to photographs.